core belief™
Bible Study Series
for junior high/middle school

THE TRUTH ABOUT
Prayer

Group

Loveland, Colorado

The Truth About Prayer

Core Belief Bible Study Series

Copyright © 1998 Group Publishing, Inc.

Credits

Editor: Karl Leuthauser
Creative Development Editors: Ivy Beckwith and Paul Woods
Chief Creative Officer: Joani Schultz
Copy Editor: Julie Meiklejohn
Art Director: Ray Tollison
Cover Art Director: Jeff A. Storm
Computer Graphic Artist: Eris Klein
Photographer: Jafe Parsons
Production Manager: Gingar Kunkel

ISBN 0-7644-0869-0

10 9 8 7 6 5 4 3 2 1   07 06 05 04 03 02 01 00 99 98

Printed in the United States of America.

Bible Study Series
for junior high/middle school

contents:

the Core Belief: Prayer

Simply put, prayer is honest communication with God. It's how we build a personal relationship with our Creator, Redeemer, Father, and Friend. It's a way of life, and it involves our entire being. More than just words we say at a specified time of day, it's the way we live our lives in constant contact with God. We can pray about anything, using a variety of means to communicate with God. We can pray by ourselves or in the company of our brothers and sisters. We can pray in Jesus' name and with the Holy Spirit's power.

And when we pray, God responds. He hears our prayers, and we can trust that he answers our prayers wisely and lovingly.

the Helpful Stuff

the ▼Studies

▼Prayer as a Core Christian Belief

If the kids in your youth group are like most teenagers, only three out of every ten of them pray daily. Even fewer—a paltry 15 percent—regard personal prayer as an important influence in their lives. Without a serious and committed prayer life, how can kids find real change in their lives? How can they form a personal relationship with the almighty God of the universe?

Fortunately, the news is not all bad: 90 percent of kids express interest in learning how to pray. Nine out of every ten members of your youth group want to pray more often and more effectively. The door is wide-open, so you can seize the opportunity and help your young people meet their most crucial need and desire, a vital relationship with their loving God.

Kids may not feel that prayer is important because they may have been disappointed by an answer (or seeming lack of an answer) they received regarding an important **prayer.** The first study in this book will help them overcome this obstacle as they learn that God communicates answers to our prayers in many different ways.

The second study will remind kids that prayer is not a one-sided conversation. God communicates with us through Scripture, circumstances, conscience, and thoughts. Kids will be encouraged as they discover that prayer needs to include **waiting,** since prayer is communication with God.

The third study will help kids explore some of the many benefits of **prayer,** including protection and comfort. This study will help kids see that prayer brings freedom from many things, including freedom from fear.

The final study of this book will demonstrate that our relationship with God is more than asking, confessing, praising, and waiting. It also includes **serving others.** As we pray, God directs us to reach out to others. As others pray, God sometimes directs us to act as answers to prayers.

When your kids discover that prayer is simply honest communication with our loving, personal God, they'll pray more often and with greater confidence. As a result, they'll love God more deeply and serve him more effectively in every area of their lives.

For a more comprehensive look at this Core Christian Belief, read **Group's *Get Real: Making Core Christian Beliefs Relevant to Teenagers.***

DEPTHFINDER

HOW THE BIBLE DESCRIBES PRAYER

To help you effectively guide your kids toward this Core Christian Belief, use these overviews as a launching point for a more in-depth study of prayer.

- **Prayer includes honest communication and personal fellowship with God.** Prayer is more than just talking to God. It is relating openly and honestly to God as our closest and most faithful friend. (Psalms 10; 18:1; Romans 8:14-16; Hebrews 4:14-16)

- **Prayer is more a lifestyle than a momentary act.** Since God is always with us, we can and should communicate with him all the time. In short, our lives should be never-ending conversations with God. (Psalm 55:16-17; Luke 18:1; Ephesians 6:18; 1 Thessalonians 5:17)

- **Prayer involves the entire person.** Because prayer is our means of relating to and communicating with God, it must be more than a mindless repetition of pious words. Authentic prayer requires the full engagement of your intellect, emotions, and will. (Deuteronomy 6:5; 1 Samuel 1:9-11; Matthew 6:7; Colossians 4:2; James 5:16)

- **We can pray to God about anything.** God is the sovereign and all-powerful ruler of the universe, so there is no problem too difficult for him. And since God loves us and lives within us, we can trust him to take seriously even our most minor concerns. (Psalms 103:13-14; 113:4-9; Matthew 7:7-11; Romans 8:26-27; Philippians 4:6)

- **There are as many types of prayer as there are types of people and circumstances.** In the Bible God authorizes many kinds of prayer, including complaint, praise, petition, thanksgiving, confession, intercession, expression of trust, and simply sharing thoughts and emotions. (Psalms 13; 30; 51; Matthew 6:9-13; 1 Timothy 2:1-4)

- **When we pray, we should trust that God will respond in a wise and loving way.** God accepts even a simple cry for help as an expression of trust in him. The only sign of a total lack of faith is the refusal to pray. (Psalms 56:1-4; 62; Matthew 7:9-11; Mark 9:24; 11:24)

- **The only inappropriate prayer is a dishonest or insincere prayer.** Since healthy relationships require honest communication, God wants us to express even negative thoughts and emotions. God knows when we're angry, confused, afraid, or weak in faith, and he loves us anyway. God wants us to talk honestly with him and rely upon him to get us through difficult times. (Psalm 88; Jeremiah 20:7-18; Matthew 6:7; Luke 18:9-14)
- **God answers our appeals in a variety of ways.** Sometimes God gives us what we ask for; other times he enables us to answer our own requests. Sometimes God asks us to wait or to accept a response different from what we had asked for. In each instance, however, God acts wisely and lovingly. (Luke 18:1-8; 2 Corinthians 12:1-10)
- **We should pray with others and by ourselves.** When we join others in prayer, we draw closer to God and to one another. However, sometimes we should pray privately to develop our private relationship with God and to avoid the temptation to call attention to ourselves (Psalm 74; 1 Kings 8:22-53; Matthew 6:5-6; Acts 2:42; 4:24)
- **We should pray to God in the name of Jesus and the power of the Holy Spirit.** Since Jesus enables us to live in fellowship with God, we can rely on him when we approach God in prayer. The Holy Spirit helps us speak to and hear from God. (John 16:23-24; 15:7, 16; Romans 8:26-27; Ephesians 5:19-20)

CORE CHRISTIAN BELIEF OVERVIEW

Here are the twenty-four Core Christian Belief categories that form the backbone of Group's Core Belief Bible Study Series:

The Nature of God	Jesus Christ	The Holy Spirit
Humanity	Evil	Suffering
Creation	The Spiritual Realm	The Bible
Salvation	Spiritual Growth	Personal Character
God's Justice	Sin & Forgiveness	The Last Days
Love	The Church	Worship
Authority	Prayer	Family
Service	Relationships	Sharing Faith

Look for Group's Core Belief Bible Study Series books in these other Core Christian Beliefs!

about

Bible Study Series
for junior high/middle school

Think for a moment about your young people. When your students walk out of your youth program after they graduate from junior high or high school, what do you want them to know? What foundation do you want them to have so they can make wise choices?

You probably want them to know the essentials of the Christian faith. You want them to base everything they do on the foundational truths of Christianity. Are you meeting this goal?

If you have any doubt that your kids will walk into adulthood knowing and living by the tenets of the Christian faith, then you've picked up the right book. All the books in Group's Core Belief Bible Study Series encourage young people to discover the essentials of Christianity and to put those essentials into practice. Let us explain...

What Is Group's Core Belief Bible Study Series?

Group's Core Belief Bible Study Series is a biblically in-depth study series for junior high and senior high teenagers. This Bible study series utilizes four defining commitments to create each study. These "plumb lines" provide structure and continuity for every activity, study, project, and discussion. They are:

● **A Commitment to Biblical Depth**—Core Belief Bible Study Series is founded on the belief that kids not only *can* understand the deeper truths of the Bible but also *want* to understand them. Therefore, the activities and studies in this series strive to explain the "why" behind every truth we explore. That way, kids learn principles, not just rules.

● **A Commitment to Relevance**—Most kids aren't interested in abstract theories or doctrines about the universe. They want to know how to live successfully right now, today, in the heat of problems they can't ignore. Because of this, each study connects a real-life need with biblical principles that speak directly to that need. This study series finally bridges the gap between Bible truths and the real-world issues kids face.

● **A Commitment to Variety**—Today's young people have been raised in a sound bite world. They demand variety. For that reason, no two meetings in this study series are shaped exactly the same.

● **A Commitment to Active and Interactive Learning**—Active learning is learning by doing. Interactive learning simply takes active learning a step further by having kids teach each other what they've learned. It's a process that helps kids internalize and remember their discoveries.

For a more detailed description of these concepts, see the section titled "Why Active and Interactive Learning Works With Teenagers" beginning on page 57.

So how can you accomplish all this in a set of four easy-to-lead Bible studies? By weaving together various "power" elements to produce a fun experience that leaves kids challenged and encouraged.

Betrayed!

HELPING KIDS DEAL WITH REJECTION FROM THE PEOPLE THEY LOVE

by Jennifer Garrell

THE POINT:

God is love.

■ Betrayal has very little shock value for this generation. It's as commonplace as compact discs and mosh pits. For many kids today, betrayal characterizes their parents' wedding vows. It's part of their curriculum at school; it defines the headlines and evening news. Betrayal is not only accepted—it's expected. ■ At the heart of such acceptance lies the belief that nothing is absolute. No vow, no law, no promise can be trusted. Relationships are betrayed at the earliest convenience. Repeatedly, kids see that something called "love" lasts just as long as it's ~~permanence. But deep inside, they hunger to see a~~

The Study AT A GLANCE

SECTION	MINUTES	WHAT STUDENTS WILL DO	SUPPLIES
Discussion Starter	up to 5	JUMP-START—Identify some of the most common themes in today's movies.	Newsprint, marker
Investigation of Betrayal	12 to 15	REALITY CHECK—Form groups to compare anonymous, real-life stories of betrayal with experiences in their own lives.	"Profiles of Betrayal" handouts (p. 20), highlighter pens, newsprint, marker, tape
	3 to 5	WHO BETRAYED WHOM?—Guess the identities of the people profiled in the handouts.	Paper, tape, pen
Investigation of True Love	15 to 18	SOURCE WORK—Study and discuss God's definition of perfect love.	Bibles, newsprint, marker
	5 to 7	LOVE MESSAGES—Create unique ways to send a "message of love" to the victims of betrayal they've been studying.	Newsprint, markers, tape
Personal Application	10 to 15	SYMBOLIC LOVE—Give a partner a personal symbol of perfect love.	Paper lunch sack, pens, scissors, paper, catalogs

notes:

● A Relevant Topic—More than ever before, kids live in the now. What matters to them and what attracts their hearts is what's happening in their world at this moment. For this reason, every Core Belief Bible Study focuses on a particular hot topic that kids care about.

● A Core Christian Belief—Group's Core Belief Bible Study Series organizes the wealth of Christian truth and experience into twenty-four Core Christian Belief categories. These twenty-four headings act as umbrellas for a collection of detailed beliefs that define Christianity and set it apart from the world and every other religion. Each book in this series features one Core Christian Belief with lessons suited for junior high or senior high students.

"But," you ask, "won't my kids be bored talking about all these spiritual beliefs?" No way! As a youth leader, you know the value of using hot topics to connect with young people. Ultimately teenagers talk about issues because they're searching for meaning in their lives. They want to find the one equation that will make sense of all the confusing events happening around them. Each Core Belief Bible Study answers that need by connecting a hot topic with a powerful Christian principle. Kids walk away from the study with something more solid than just the shifting ebb and flow of their own opinions. They walk away with a deeper understanding of their Christian faith.

● The Point—This simple statement is designed to be the intersection between the Core Christian Belief and the hot topic. Everything in the study ultimately focuses on The Point so that kids study it and allow it time to sink into their hearts.

● The Study at a Glance—A quick look at this chart will tell you what kids will do, how long it will take them to do it, and what supplies you'll need to get it done.

The Bible Connection—This is the power base of each study. Whether it's just one verse or several chapters, The Bible Connection provides the vital link between kids' minds and their hearts. The content of each Core Belief Bible Study reflects the belief that the true power of God—the power to expose, heal, and change kids' lives—is contained in his Word.

THE POINT OF *BETRAYED!*:

God is love.

THE BIBLE CONNECTION

 1 JOHN 4:7-21   The Apostle John explains the nature and definition of perfect love.

In this study, kids will compare the imperfect love defined in real-life stories of betrayal to God's definition of perfect love.

By making this comparison, kids can discover that God is love and therefore incapable of betraying them. Then they'll be able to recognize the incredible opportunity God off[...] relationship worthy of their absolute trust.

Explore the verses in The Bible Connection [...] mation in the Depthfinder boxes throughout [...] understanding of how these Scriptures conne[...]

LEADER TIP

THE STUDY

DISCUSSION STARTER ▼

Jump-Start (up to 5 minutes) As kids arrive, ask them to think[...] common themes in movies, books, TV show[...] have kids each contribute ideas for a mast[...] two other kids in the room and sharing [...] sider providing copies of People maga[...] what's currently showing on television [...] their suggestions, write their respon[...] **come up with a lot of great ide[...] ent, look through this list and [...] ments most of these themes [...]**

After kids make several su[...] responses are connected w[...]

● **Why do you think [...]**

Betrayed! 17

LEADER TIP for The Study Because this topic can be so powerful and relevant to kids' lives, your group members may be tempted to get caught up in issues and lose sight of the deeper biblical principle found in The Point. Help your kids grasp The Point by guiding kids to focus on the biblical investigation and discussing how God's truth connects with reality in their lives.

DEPTHFINDER UNDERSTANDING INTEGRITY

Your students may not be entirely familiar with the meaning of integrity, especially as it might apply to God's character in the Trinity. Use these definitions (taken from Webster's II New Riverside Dictionary) and other information to help you guide kids toward a better understanding of how God maintains integrity through the three expressions of the Trinity.

Integrity: 1. Firm adherence to a code or standard of values. 2. The state of being unimpaired. 3. The quality or condition of being undivided.

Synonyms for integrity include probity, completeness, wholeness, soundness, and perfection.

Our word "integrity" comes from the Latin word *integritas*, which means soundness. *Integritas* is also the root of the word "integer," which means "whole or complete," as in a "whole" number.

The Hebrew word that's often translated "integrity" (for example, in Psalm 25:21 [NIV]) is *tam.* It means whole, perfect, sincere, and honest.

CREATIVE GOD-EXPLORATION ▼

Top Hats (18 to 20 minutes) Form three groups, with each trio member from the previous activity going to a different group. Give each group Bibles, paper, and pens, and assign each group a different hat God wears: Father, Son, or Holy Spirit. [...] their goal is to write one list describing what God does in the [...] God's character.

Depthfinder Boxes—These informative sidelights located throughout each study add insight into a particular passage, word, historical fact, or Christian doctrine. Depthfinder boxes also provide insight into teen culture, adolescent development, current events, and philosophy.

● **Leader Tips**—These handy information boxes coach you through the study, offering helpful suggestions on everything from altering activities for different-sized groups to streamlining discussions to using effective discipline techniques.

holy Profiles

Your assigned Bible passage describes how a particular person or group responded when confronted with God's holiness. Use the information in your passage to help your group discuss the questions below. Then use your flashlights to teach the other two groups what you discover.

■ Based on your passage, what does holiness look like?

■ What does holiness sound like?

■ When people see God's holiness, how does it affect them?

■ How is this response to God's holiness like humility?

■ Based on your passage, how would you describe humility?

■ Why is humility an appropriate human response to God's holiness?

■ Based on what you see in your passage, do you think you are a humble person? Why or why not?

■ What's one way you could develop humility in your life this week?

● **Handouts**—Most Core Belief Bible Studies include photocopiable handouts to use with your group. Handouts might take the form of a fun game, a lively discussion starter, or a challenging study page for kids to take home— anything to make your study more meaningful and effective.

The Last Word on Core Belief Bible Studies

Soon after you begin to use Group's Core Belief Bible Study Series, you'll see signs of real growth in your group members. Your kids will gain a deeper understanding of the Bible and of their own Christian faith. They'll see more clearly how a relationship with Jesus affects their daily lives. And they'll grow closer to God.

But that's not all. You'll also see kids grow closer to one another.

That's because this series is founded on the principle that Christian faith grows best in the context of relationship. Each study uses a variety of interactive pairs and small groups and always includes discussion questions that promote deeper relationships. The friendships kids will build through this study series will enable them to grow *together* toward a deeper relationship with God.

LISTEN UP

Learning to Hear God's Answers to Prayer

.... by Lisa Baba Lauffer

■ Telephones, e-mail, television, answering machines, videos, fax machines, beepers, computer chat rooms—how many ways can we communicate a message these days? We have access to amazing and mystifying technology, enabling us to communicate with people around the planet almost instantly. And our junior high kids expertly navigate their way through this maze of technology—it's as natural to them as breathing. ■ Within this context of instantaneous communication, waiting for God to speak is *not* natural for junior highers. Our kids expect immediate results, but God doesn't communicate with us at the push of a button. ■ Nevertheless, God *does* speak. In his perfect timing and ways, God answers our prayers. He listens to our needs and waits for us to slow down long enough to hear him. ■ This study emphasizes listening for the many ways God communicates his answers to our prayers.

THE POINT:

God communicates answers to our prayers in many different ways.

The Study
AT A GLANCE

SECTION	MINUTES	WHAT STUDENTS WILL DO	SUPPLIES
Learning Game	15 to 20	BLAH, BLAH, BLAH—Communicate with each other by speaking only the word "blah."	
Relational Time	10 to 15	HEAR ME OUT—Practice active listening with a partner. Share what they like about being heard.	
Four-Way Bible Exploration	10 to 15	WHEN GOD SPEAKS, PEOPLE LISTEN—Use creative groups to explore how God answered prayers in Scripture.	Bibles
	5 to 10	WHAT DID YOU HEAR?—Discuss how each group's creative communication reflects God's communication with us.	Bibles, newsprint, marker
Creative Prayer	up to 5	SILENT TIME—Spend time in silence before God.	Bibles, paper, pencils

notes:

God communicates answers to our prayer in many different ways.

THE BIBLE CONNECTION

GENESIS 15:1-6	God answers Abram's prayer by speaking to him.
JUDGES 6:33-40	God answers Gideon's prayer by making some wool wet, then dry.
DANIEL 2:17-19	God answers Daniel's prayer by giving him a vision.
JOHN 11:38-44	God answers Jesus' prayer by raising Lazarus from the dead.

I n this study, kids will use two creative experiences to explore how they communicate with each other and how God communicates with them. Then they will compare what they learn to Bible passages describing ways God communicated answers to prayers in biblical times.

Through this exploration, kids can discover how to listen to God's answers to their prayers today.

Explore the verses in The Bible Connection, then study the information in the Depthfinder boxes throughout the study to gain a deeper understanding of how these Scriptures connect with your young people.

LEADER TIP for The Study

Because this topic can be so powerful and relevant to kids' lives, your group members may be tempted to get caught up in issues and lose sight of the deeper biblical principle found in The Point. Help your kids grasp The Point by focusing on the biblical investigation and discussing how God's truth connects with reality in their lives.

THE STUDY

LEARNING GAME ▼

LEADER TIP for Blah, Blah, Blah

While you're explaining this activity to the Communicators, provide a place for the Followers to wait. Assign a volunteer leader to stay with the Followers and discuss these questions:
● When were you a really good listener for someone who needed you?
● How did you know that you understood what that person said?

LEADER TIP for The Study

Whenever you tell groups to discuss a list of questions, write the questions on newsprint and tape the newsprint to the wall so each group can answer the questions at its own pace.

Blah, Blah, Blah (15 to 20 minutes) When everyone has arrived, have students form trios. Say: **We're going to play a communication game. Choose two people in your trio to be Communicators. The third person will be the Follower.** Send all of the Followers out of the room with an adult leader. Make sure the Followers can't hear you.

While the Followers are out of the room, say: **In a moment I'm going to give you a scenario to act out with your Followers when they come back in. But your Followers won't know what the scenario is. You'll need to communicate the scenario to your Followers so they can imitate you and then describe the scenario to you in their own words. But there's a catch. Repeat after me: "Blah."** (Have kids repeat "blah" to you.) **The only word you may speak to your Followers is "blah." You can act out the scenario using whatever motions you like, but when you speak, substitute the word "blah" for the words you'd use in your sentences.**

Demonstrate this activity by using the word "blah" to get one of your students to shake your hand and sit in a chair. Use the word "blah" as a substitute for every word you'd use in a sentence, using the same cadence in your voice as you would in that sentence. For example, when extending your hand for the student to shake, instead of saying, "How nice to meet you," say, "Blah blah blah blah blah" with the same inflection.

Once kids understand how the activity works, say: **I'm going to call in the Followers soon. Using "blah blahs" and appropriate physical gestures, you must get your Followers to act out this scenario. They must pretend to put on Rollerblades, create a pizza in a kitchen, and deliver the pizza to me. When your trio completes the scenario, have your Followers describe to you what they just did.**

Call in the Followers, and say: **Followers, return to your trios. Your Communicators are going to get you to act out a scenario. But they can't say any words except "blah, blah, blah." Pay attention to their actions and any other ways they choose to communicate with you. While you're doing this activity, think about what helps you understand your Communicators. Also, be prepared to describe the scenario when you've completed it. Communicators, do your job!**

Have trios act out their scenarios. When all of the trios have accomplished the task, say: **Communicators, have your Followers tell you what they just acted out. Help them describe the activity accurately by giving hints when they need it.**

When all of the Followers have accurately described the pizza-making scenario, say: **Good job! You've just communicated with one another to accomplish a task together. In your trios, answer the following questions:**

  ● **What's your reaction to this activity?**
  ● **What did you discover about communication through this activity?**
  ● **How's this activity like the ways God communicates to us when he's answering our prayers?**

Say: <u>**God communicates answers to our prayers in**</u>  <u>**many different ways**</u>. Today we're going to explore how he communicates with us and learn how to listen to him more effectively.

RELATIONAL TIME ▼

Hear Me Out
(10 to 15 minutes)
Form pairs and then say: **Let's do another activity to help us learn how to listen to God. In your pairs, designate one partner as the Communicator and the other as the Listener. I'm going to give the Communicator one minute to talk about a topic. The Listener's job is to just listen for that minute. Don't respond with your own opinions or feelings about what the Communicator said. Just listen. When time is up, the Listener will have one minute to repeat what the Communicator said. Then we'll switch roles and repeat the experience. Communicators, you have one minute to share about a time when someone really listened to you.**

Give the Communicators one minute to share and then give the Listeners one minute to repeat what they heard. Say: **Communicators, while your Listeners repeat what you said, help them succeed in understanding you. If they didn't quite hear everything**

LEADER TIP
for Hear Me Out
Many kids will run out of things to say after thirty seconds. Encourage students to continue listening quietly for the full minute, even if their partners stop talking.

DEPTH FINDER — UNDERSTANDING THE BIBLE

When we don't listen to God, the results can be disastrous. Not only do we pay the "real world" consequences for our disobedience, we breach our relationship with God.

If you want to know more about how God responded when his people didn't listen to him, check out these Old Testament passages:

  ● Numbers 13:1–14:24 (God forbade the Israelites from entering the Promised Land.)
  ● Numbers 20:2-12 (God denied Moses the privilege of leading the Israelites into the Promised Land.)
  ● Joshua 7:1-26 (God allowed the people of Ai to defeat the Israelites.)
  ● Daniel 4:24-33 (God caused King Nebuchadnezzar to live like an animal for seven years.)

you said, tell them again what you said and give them another chance to communicate what they heard.

After one minute, have kids switch roles and repeat the activity.

Have each pair find another pair, forming a foursome, and discuss these questions:

● **How did you feel when your partner listened to you without immediately responding?**

● **What's your reaction to concentrating on someone's words without responding right away?**

● **How does listening like this affect your relationship with your partner?**

● **How is this activity like praying about something and then listening for God's answer to your prayers?**

Say: **Listening is an important part of our relationships, including our relationship with God. When we pray for something, we need to really listen for God's answers, because** <u>God communicates answers to our prayers in many different ways</u>. **We're going to explore some of those ways in the next activity.**

FOUR-WAY BIBLE EXPLORATION ▼

When God Speaks, People Listen
(10 to 15 minutes)

Say: **We're going to delve into the Bible to find some ways God has answered people's prayers in the past.**

Form four groups, and number the groups from one to four. A group can be one person. Assign each group the appropriate Scripture passage below:

● Group 1—Genesis 15:1-6 (God answers Abram's prayer by telling him he will have a son.)

● Group 2—Judges 6:33-40 (God answers Gideon's prayer by making some wool wet, then dry.)

● Group 3—Daniel 2:17-19 (God answers Daniel's prayer by revealing to him King Nebuchadnezzar's dream and its meaning.)

● Group 4—John 11:38-44 (God answers Jesus' prayer by raising Lazarus from the dead.)

Say: **In your groups, read your Scripture passage aloud. As you read your passage, look for the way God answered someone's prayer.**

When groups have finished reading, assign each group the appropriate communication mode listed below:

● Group 1—Have the group develop a sentence that summarizes the passage, divide the sentence among group members, and assign each group member to shout his or her part of the sentence from a different area of the room.

● Group 2—Have the group develop a sentence that summarizes the passage; have them explain the passage without using the words "wool," "wet," "dry," "morning," or "ground"; and have the other groups guess what happened.

● Group 3—Have the group develop a sentence that summarizes the passage and have all group members speak at once, simultaneously explaining the passage in their own words.

● Group 4—Have the group develop a sentence that summarizes the passage and have them move among the class members and whisper the sentence in class members' ears.

When all the groups understand their assignments, give them five minutes to read through their assigned passages, create a presentation about the passage based on your instructions, and practice.

After the groups practice, have each group give its presentation. Congratulate kids for their efforts.

"He urged them to plead for mercy from the God of heaven concerning this mystery, so that he and his friends might not be executed with the rest of the wise men of Babylon. During the night the mystery was revealed to Daniel in a vision. Then Daniel praised the God of heaven"

—Daniel 2:18-19

What Did You Hear? (5 to 10 minutes)

Have kids form foursomes by finding one member from each group. Say: **Think of something you recently prayed for, such as healing for yourself or someone close to you, getting a good grade, or being safe in a dangerous situation. Tell your group what your prayer request was and if God has answered it yet. If he has, tell your group what God's answer was.**

Have group members share their requests with one another. Then ask:

● **How are the ways we communicated about our Bible passages like or unlike the ways God communicates his answers to our prayers?** Have foursomes share their answers to this question with the larger group. Write their answers on newsprint.

● **Based on your own experience, what are other ways God might communicate answers to prayer?** Have foursomes share their answers to this question. Write their answers on newsprint.

● **Do you think God answers your prayers? Why or why not?**

● **How do you respond when God answers one of your prayers?**

● **How does knowing that God answers your prayers affect your view of him? affect your relationship with him?**

Say: **As we've seen in the Bible stories we explored and in our discussion, <u>God communicates answers to our prayers in many different ways</u>. We can hear his answers through Scripture, through creation, or through a friend's words. Whatever way he chooses to communicate with us, we need to listen to him, even when he's hard to hear or when he's saying something we don't want to hear.**

Let's practice listening to God right now.

DEPTHFINDER — UNDERSTANDING THESE KIDS

"**Why should we?**" Your kids may respond with that question when you teach them about listening to God. God is the ultimate authority figure, and today's kids feel that authority figures have let them down. Author Douglas Rushkoff states that young people today "don't want to rally behind any authority figure lest that authority figure resigns or turns out to be untrue." For some kids, this disenchantment has developed from personal, painful disappointment at the hands of authority figures such as their parents, teachers, and coaches. When burned, these young people quickly learn not to trust again.

But God never lets anyone down. You know that, and your kids need to learn it. They need to understand that they can trust God to answer their prayers perfectly.

Encourage your kids to read Matthew 7:9-11. Then have your kids consider one way they've seen God provide a good thing for them, such as a new friend when they were lonely or a sense of peace during a crisis. Then challenge your students to pray for something they need and actively look for God's answer, reminding them that the answer they receive is God's best for them.

CREATIVE PRAYER ▼

LEADER TIP for Silent Time

Write the four "Silent Time" questions on newsprint for kids to refer to during their prayer experience.

Silent Time

(up to 5 minutes)

Have students take their Bibles and find a private spot in the room.

Say: **For the next three minutes, pray silently. Ask God to communicate an answer to one of your prayers. You can start this time by asking God to quiet your heart. Then, as you pray silently, ask him:**

- **What do you want to say to me?**
- **What do I need most from you?**
- **What do you want to give me?**
- **What do you want me to look at in Scripture?**

After three minutes, give each student paper and a pencil. Say: **On your paper, write words or phrases that reflect what you think God is saying to you, how you feel about this prayer experience, or how you feel about your relationship with God.**

Kids may write things such as, "I hear God telling me to be kind to my sister," "I feel frustrated because I can't hear God," or "I feel like God is near me."

After the prayer experience, challenge kids to keep their papers with them, in a pocket or wallet, until they have taken time to pray more about their questions, issues, and feelings.

Quiet

BY JIM HAWLEY

D O W N

HELPING KIDS LEARN TO WAIT ON GOD

■ Waiting. Thinking about that word makes us cringe. Many of us get upset if we have to wait more than five minutes in the drive-through line at the fast-food restaurant. Our world promises instant gratification— quick food, quick money, quick romance, quick information. Is it any wonder that we hate to wait? ■ It's easy to see how cultural conditioning has affected the spiritual lives of teenagers. Their prayers often become rushed "to do" lists for God. ■ But God knows that most of the valuable things in life take time. Things like character, intimacy, and wisdom can't be instantly manufactured. Fortunately, God loves us enough to refrain from answering our prayers according to our hurried timetables. God answers our prayers according to his plan. God encourages us to wait for his will while we work on developing an intimate relationship with him. ■ Use this study to help kids explore the deeper meaning of prayer. Help kids learn to wait on God so that they can move beyond the idea of God as a benevolent benefactor and begin to understand God as a compassionate and intimate Father.

THE POINT:

Prayer is communicating with God.

The Study
AT A GLANCE

SECTION	MINUTES	WHAT STUDENTS WILL DO	SUPPLIES
Reflective Opening	10 to 15	SEND A PRAYER—Write prayer letters, and explore their feelings about waiting for prayers to be answered.	Paper, envelopes, pens, a shoe box
Learning Activity	10 to 15	MUSICAL PEOPLE—Compete to move a group of chairs according to different instructions.	Bibles, "Chairs" handout (p. 33), scissors, chairs
Bible Exploration	15 to 20	FOUR STEPS OF PRAYER—Explore different sections of Psalm 130, and report findings to the group.	Bibles, "Psalm 130: A Prayer" handout (pp. 34-35), scissors, pens, newsprint, tape, marker
Reflective Closing	10 to 15	TIME WITH GOD—Be silent before God and pray.	Bibles, envelopes from "Send a Prayer" activity, paper, pens, stamps

notes:

THE POINT OF "QUIET DOWN":

Prayer is communicating with God.

THE BIBLE CONNECTION

PSALM 130	The psalmist waits for the Lord's salvation.
HABUKKUK 2:20	Because the Lord is holy, people are silent before him.

I n this study, kids will explore their feelings about waiting, experience confusing directions, and examine Psalm 130 before waiting for and praying to God.

Through these experiences, kids can discover how waiting can enrich their prayer lives and how prayer can help deepen their relationships with God.

Explore the verses in The Bible Connection, then examine the information in the Depthfinder boxes throughout the study to gain a deeper understanding of how these Scriptures connect with your young people.

LEADER TIP for The Study

Because this topic can be so powerful and relevant to kids' lives, your group members may be tempted to get caught up in issues and lose sight of the deeper biblical principle found in The Point. Help your kids grasp The Point by guiding kids to focus on the biblical investigation and discussing how God's truth connects with reality in their lives.

BEFORE THE STUDY

For the "Musical People" activity, gather at least one chair for each student. Make one copy of the "Chairs" handout (p. 33), and cut the sections apart.

For the "Four Steps of Prayer" activity, make one copy of the "Psalm 130: A Prayer" handout (pp. 34-35), and cut the sections apart.

THE STUDY

REFLECTIVE OPENING ▼

Send a Prayer (10 to 15 minutes)

After kids arrive, give each student a sheet of paper, a pen, and an envelope. Set a shoe box in the middle of the room. Say: **I want you to think about some prayer needs you have right now. Using the supplies provided, take a few minutes to write a prayer letter to God. After you finish your letter, fold it and stick it in an envelope—but don't seal it. Next address the letter to yourself. Finally, put your letter in this "mailbox."**

Give students a few minutes to complete and "mail" their prayer letters. Then ask:

● **What were you thinking about as you wrote your prayers?**
● **What did you think about "mailing" your prayers?**
● **How long will it take for you to get your letter if it is mailed tomorrow?**
● **How is waiting on your mail like waiting for your prayers to be answered? How is it unlike waiting?**

Have kids form pairs.

Say: **Waiting on answers to prayers may be easier for some than it is for others. When I ask you the next three questions, choose a facial expression that best shows how you feel about each question. For example, if the answer is very hard for you, you could grimace in pain. Then explain your answer to your partner.**

Have students share expressions and responses with each other as you ask the following questions:

● **Is it difficult for you to wait for most things, such as food at the drive-through or tickets to a movie?**
● **Is it difficult for you to wait for your prayers to be answered?**
● **Is it difficult for you to wait for God's direction?**

After kids share, say: **Waiting is often difficult, especially when it involves things that are important to us. Today we're going to look at different elements of prayer, including waiting. We'll discover why it's important to understand how <u>prayer is communicating with God</u>.**

LEARNING ACTIVITY ▼

Musical People (10 to 15 minutes)

Put the chairs you gathered before the study in one area of your meeting space. Have kids form three numbered groups, and give each group its portion of the "Chairs" handout (p. 33).

DEPTH FINDER
UNDERSTANDING THE BIBLE

Psalm 130 is one of seven psalms that are classified as penitential psalms. The psalm begins with a lament (verses 1-2) as the psalmist expresses his dire situation. Confession of sin follows in verses 3-4, with confidence in the Lord's mercy and forgiveness. The psalm then shifts to waiting for the Lord in verses 5-6. The waiting is emphasized through repetition. Finally, the psalmist reveals his confidence in redemption in verses 7-8. The focus moves beyond personal salvation to include all the people of Israel in the psalm's conclusion.

(Source: The Expositor's Bible Commentary, Volume 5)

For example, Group 1 will get the "Group 1" section of the handout and Group 2 will get the "Group 2" section of the handout. Have kids discuss with their groups how they can best carry out the tasks described on their handouts.

Point to the cluster of chairs, and say: **Each group is to arrange all these chairs according to the instructions on its handout. While you move the chairs, yell out the words on your handout. Only one person may move any one chair at a time. Once a person has moved a chair, he or she must find another chair to move. Once a chair has been moved, it may be moved again. If two people arrive at a chair at the same time, they must figure out who gets to move the chair. Ready? Go!**

Give kids a few minutes to play the game. After a few minutes, have kids form groups of three, with one student from each of the three original groups included in each trio. Have groups discuss the following questions:

● **Is there any way that all of the groups could have accomplished their goals? Explain.**

● **How was the work of the other groups like the distractions in your prayer life? How was it different?**

● **What things interrupt your ability to pray?**

● **What things interrupt your ability to "hear" God's direction?**

● **Read Habakkuk 2:20. How could waiting and being silent change your prayer life?**

● **What part does waiting and being silent play in your relationship with God?**

● **Why does God want us to be silent before him? to wait on him?**

Say: **The commotion of life can confuse our relationship with God. We have so many things we need to get done and so many goals we want to accomplish. Without a clear focus, our prayers can become chaotic and confused. Prayer is communicating with God. Silence, waiting, and reflection are important parts of that communication. When we are still and silent before God, he gives us a clear focus for our lives and prayers.**

LEADER TIP

for Four Steps of Prayer

Psalm 130 is being used as a model prayer for this study. The eight verses neatly divide into four aspects of prayer. Each group will study two verses, and groups will share their study insights to help kids see how the four elements of this prayer form a model prayer. The four elements of this prayer are: verses 1-2 (asking), verses 3-4 (confessing), verses 5-6 (waiting), and verses 7-8 (trusting).

Four Steps of Prayer

(15 to 20 minutes) Have kids form four numbered groups. Give each group its portion of the "Psalm 130: A Prayer" handout (pp. 34-35), a pen, and a Bible.

Say: **We can look at Psalm 130 as a guideline for focused prayer. It contains four important elements of prayer—asking, confessing, waiting, and trusting. Each group will be responsible for learning about one part of this psalm. Decide who in your group will read the psalm, who will ask the questions on the handout, who will write your group's responses on the handout, and who will share your group's responses with the other groups. Everyone else in each group can answer questions or offer ideas. After all the groups have completed the handouts, we'll hear each group's responses and see how this psalm can help you pray.**

While kids work, tape a sheet of newsprint to the wall. After a few minutes, have Group 1 share its responses. Ask for a volunteer to write the group's responses on the sheet of newsprint. Continue this process with the other three groups. Then ask:

● **Which of the four steps of this prayer come easy to you? Which are difficult for you? Explain.**

● **Which of these four steps are most important to you? Explain.**

● **What purpose does waiting serve for the psalmist?**

● **What purpose does waiting serve in prayer?**

DEPTHFINDER   UNDERSTANDING THESE KIDS

In his book, *Understanding Today's Youth Culture*, Walt Mueller describes the different challenges that today's adolescents face:

1. Growing teen violence—Guns figure significantly in teen mortality. Homicide by firearms is the number one cause of death for fifteen- to nineteen-year-old African-Americans and the second-leading cause of death among whites of the same age.

2. Pressure—One sixteen-year-old girl was representative of the responses to the author's survey when she ranked the top five pressures she felt as follows: (1) looks, (2) grades, (3) drinking, (4) sex, and (5) popularity.

3. Changing families—Teens are caught up in a number of changes in their families. Mueller lists five:

● The increase and acceptance of divorce
● One-third of this nation's families do not have fathers at home
● Increasing number of mothers working outside the home
● Decreasing amount of time parents spend with children
● Increasing family violence against children and teens

These facts demonstrate why teens have difficulty finding times of quiet in their lives. But they also point out how important it is for teens today to be able to find refuge in God. In some kids' lives, this refuge may be the only kind they can find.

DEPTHFINDER — ABOUT WAITING

Henri Nouwen was a Catholic priest and a prolific author. In *The Way of the Heart*, he explored the lives of the "Desert Fathers and Mothers" of the fourth and fifth centuries. Since the great persecutions had ended, they couldn't be witnesses for Christ through dying as martyrs. They believed they were called to flee the darkness of this world and devote their lives wholeheartedly to God . Their service included writing spiritual commentaries, counseling visitors, and making a commitment to an ascetic lifestyle. Using the story of a Roman senator who tells of God's voice instructing him to "flee, be silent, pray always, for these are the sources of sinlessness," Nouwen explains that these three concepts summarize the spirituality of the desert.

Although the spiritual discipline of prayer is obvious to all Christians, the concepts of solitude and silence are much less understood and much less practiced. Nouwen shows convincingly how solitude and silence *can* be practiced in the hectic lives of people today. Escaping the world is not the goal; connecting with God's Spirit is.

Say: **Since <u>prayer is communicating with God</u>, it's important to pray about our true feelings and concerns. It's also important to wait and be silent during prayer. Waiting can help us organize our thoughts. It also gives God an opportunity to bring things to our minds that we should pray about. For example, when you ask God to show you if you have sins to confess, it's important to wait for a minute to see if he brings anything to mind. God may not "talk" to you while you wait, but he will draw near to you and help you grow.**

REFLECTIVE CLOSING ▼

Time With God (10 to 15 minutes)
Distribute paper and pens to the students. Have kids retrieve their letters from the mailbox used in the "Send a Prayer" activity and scatter apart as much as your room allows.

Say: **Read your prayer again. I'd like you to write an additional prayer or maybe even rewrite your first prayer. Before you start writing, I'd like you to ask God to give you direction for your prayer and then wait in silence for three minutes. Use that time to think, collect your thoughts, and see if God brings anything to mind. Maybe God will bring sins to your mind you need to confess, or maybe he will bring others to mind that you should pray for. Maybe it will just be a time to focus on God. Begin waiting now.**

After three minutes, instruct kids to write their prayers. Encourage kids to silently pray their prayer letters to God. After kids have prayed, ask them to write the following questions on their letters:

● In what way has this prayer been answered?

● Has God changed my attitude concerning the situation?
● How is God working in my life?

Give each student a stamp. Say: **Seal and stamp your letter, and put it in this mailbox. I will mail the letter to you. When you get your letter in a few days, open it and think about the questions you wrote on your letter. Then spend some time praying. Thank God for how you've learned more about how <u>prayer is communicating with God.</u>**

On your way home, drop the letters in a mailbox.

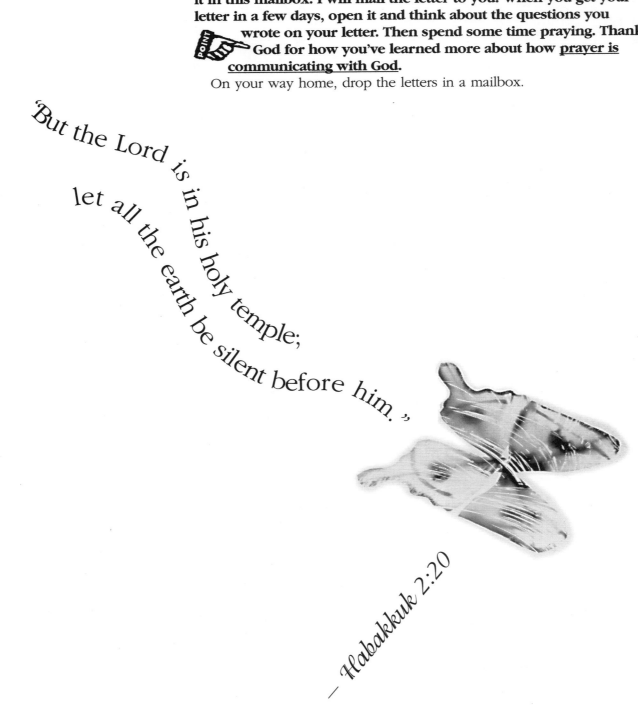

"But the Lord is in his holy temple; let all the earth be silent before him."

— Habakkuk 2:20

C·H·A·I·R·S

....

GROUP 1

CHAIR MOVERS' TASK: *Put all the chairs in a circle.*

CHAIR MOVERS' CHANT: *"We're the round-'em-up chair movers!"*

....

GROUP 2

CHAIR MOVERS' TASK: *Put all the chairs along the walls.*

CHAIRS MOVERS' CHANT: *"We're the up-against-the-wall chair movers!"*

....

Group 3

CHAIR MOVERS' TASK: *Put all the chairs in lines or rows.*

CHAIR MOVERS' CHANT: *"We're the row-row-row-your-chair chair movers!"*

....

PSALM 130: *A Prayer*

GROUP 1

Psalm 130 gives us a model for prayer. The first step in this model is **asking.** Read Psalm 130:1-2.

- What is the person in this psalm asking God for?

- How is asking an important part of prayer?

- How has asking God for something in your prayers been helpful for you?

● ●

GROUP 2

Psalm 130 gives us a model for prayer. The second step in this model is **confessing.** Read Psalm 130:3-4.

- What is being confessed in this psalm?

- How is confession an important part of prayer?

- In your prayers, how has confession been helpful for you?

GROUP 3

Psalm 130 gives us a model for prayer. The third step in this model is **waiting.** Read Psalm 130:5-6.

● How is waiting demonstrated in this psalm?

● How is waiting an important part of prayer?

● In your prayers, how has the element of waiting been helpful for you?

● ●

GROUP 4

Psalm 130 gives us a model for prayer. The fourth step in this model is **trusting.** Read Psalm 130:7-8.

● How is trust expressed in this psalm?

● How is trusting an important part of prayer?

● In your prayers, how has the attitude of trust been helpful for you?

FEAR NOT

Helping
Kids
Face
Life
With
Courage

BY JENNIFER ROOT WILGER

❋ AIDS. ❋ Gangs. ❋ Guns in schools. ❋ Rising crime rates. ❋ Drive-by shootings. ❋ Terrifying challenges face this generation of young people. The potential for personal harm is great enough to tempt even the compassionate and caring to lock themselves in their homes, pull the shades, and check out from life altogether. Hiding in fear is no way to live. ❋ This study helps young people explore their fears, examine their responses to fear, and discover how they can cope with fear through prayer.

THE POINT:

Prayer can free you from your fears.

The Study
AT A GLANCE

SECTION	MINUTES	WHAT STUDENTS WILL DO	SUPPLIES
Discussion Starters	10 to 15	FEARS ALL AROUND ME—Write their thoughts about fear on newsprint taped to the walls.	Newsprint, tape, black markers
	5 to 10	A DAY IN THE LIFE OF A FEAR—Restrict each other's movements and then act out a day's activities.	Masking tape, scissors
Digging In	10 to 12	WHEN I'M AFRAID—Read a few psalms, and apply them to their own fears.	Bibles, "Psalms" Depthfinders (p. 43), green markers
	10 to 12	PRAY IT!—Write their own psalms about their fears.	Bibles, "Psalms" Depthfinders (p. 43), green and black markers, newsprint
Response	5 to 10	CUT LOOSE—Wrap themselves in string and then free each other from it as someone reads Scriptures.	Bibles, string, scissors
Closing	up to 5	TEARING DOWN THE FEARS—Tear the newsprint from the walls.	Bibles, masking tape, basket

notes:

THE POINT OF "FEAR NOT":

Prayer can free you from your fears.

THE BIBLE CONNECTION

DEUTERONOMY 31:6, 8; PSALM 3:3, 6; PSALM 27:1-3; PSALM 118:5-6; ISAIAH 41:13; and JOHN 14:27	These passages help us deal with fear.
PSALMS 3; 27:7-10; 37:1-19; 43; 46; 55; and 91	These psalms describe God's nearness and power in the midst of frightening situations.
2 TIMOTHY 1:7	Paul writes that God gives us a spirit of power.

I n this study, kids will creatively journal and explore their experiences with fear. They'll also read psalms and learn about God's nearness in frightening situations—then create their own psalms to pray when they feel afraid.

Through their writing and exploration, kids can discover how to conquer their fears by praying.

Explore the verses in The Bible Connection, then examine the information in the Depthfinder boxes throughout the study to gain a deeper understanding of how these Scriptures connect with your young people.

BEFORE THE STUDY

For the "Fears All Around Me" activity, cover all four walls of your meeting room by taping newsprint from the ceiling to the floor. You'll cover the walls more quickly if you use a roll of newsprint instead of newsprint sheets. Many local newspapers will donate the ends of their newsprint rolls.

THE STUDY

DISCUSSION STARTERS ▼

Fears All Around Me (10 to 15 minutes)

As kids arrive, assign each of them one of the walls you prepared before the study and distribute black markers. Say: **Throughout our meeting, you'll "free-write" about today's topic. Before I give you the topic, let me explain how free-writing works. When I announce a subject or question, you'll respond by writing on the newsprint whatever comes to your mind. There's only one rule in free-writing: your pen must be moving on the newsprint at all times. If your first reaction to a topic or question is "umm" or "I don't know" or "Why do we have to answer this question?" write that down. Perhaps your first thought will be a picture. If so, draw it. Free-write the first thing you think of, and continue to record whatever thoughts come to your mind as you write.**

From time to time, others will read what you've written. You don't have to put your name on anything you write, but please avoid writing anything vulgar or offensive.

Answer questions kids might have about free-writing and then continue: **Our topic today is fear. We'll do four free-writes right now and discuss the last one with a partner.**

Have kids complete the following sentences. Allow no more than one minute for kids to write their responses. Before you read each sentence, warn kids that they have ten seconds to finish writing their responses to the previous one.

- **The color of fear is...because...**
- **When I was a kid, I was most afraid of...**
- **When I was a kid, I responded to fear by...**
- **Today I respond to fear by...**

When kids have finished, say: **Turn to a partner and read to each other your free-writes about how you respond to fear today. Then compare your responses, and discuss how they're alike or different.**

After one minute, invite pairs to report their fear responses to the larger group.

Say: **We all respond to our fears in different ways. Some people choose to run from their fears. Let's experience what that might feel like.**

Have kids stand near one of the childhood fears they've written on the newsprint. Then say: **Read your fear aloud and then run to the wall on your left. Search the fears written on that wall. If you see a fear that would have scared you as a child or would scare you now, read it aloud and run to the next wall on your left. If you don't see anything that would have scared you then or now, quickly write a** one- or two-word childhood fear, such as "big dogs" or "the dark." Then run from it to the next wall. Continue around the room until you've written several childhood fears on each wall.

Let kids run around the room three or four times. Then have them form trios to discuss these questions:

● **What's your reaction to running from the fears on the walls?**

● **How is running from those fears like the way you usually handle fear? How is it different?**

● **As long as you stayed in this room, you were caught in a cycle of fear, running from wall to wall. How is this like the way fear affects you in real life? How is it different?**

● **How might you break the cycle of fear?**

Say: **There's a lot to fear these days, and sometimes you might feel surrounded by fear. But today you'll learn how <u>prayer can free you from your fears</u>.**

A Day in the Life of a Fear (5 to 10 minutes)

Say: **We've just taken a fun look at our fears. Let's now focus on what we fear today**.

Form trios, and have each trio find a section of newsprint to write on. Give each trio a roll of masking tape. Say: **In your trios, name three things you're afraid of. As you name each fear, write it on the newsprint. Then the other members of your trio will wrap three tape bands around you—one for each fear you wrote. You'll choose where to be taped. For example, you could have your arms, wrists, fingers, legs, or feet taped together. Make sure you wrap the tape around enough times that it won't break.**

As kids wrap tape around each other, circulate among the trios to assist them. When two members in each trio have been taped, they'll need help taping the third person.

When trios have finished, say: **I'm going to read a list of activities that you probably do each day. After I read each activity, act it out while you are still taped up. As you do this, think of how acting out these activities while bound by tape is like living through a day bound by fear.**

Read the following list of daily activities, and give kids fifteen seconds to act out each one:

● **You arrive at school and open your locker.**

● **You go to class.**

● **You write a note to a friend.**

● **You eat lunch.**

● **You go to PE.**

● **You go home and do your homework.**

● **You get ready for bed.**

Then say: **I'm going to ask you three questions to discuss in your trios. As you discuss each question, you may each remove one tape band.** Provide scissors for kids to use when removing their tape bands. Ask:

LEADER TIP for A Day in the Life of a Fear

If the kids in your group usually wear nice clothes to church, you may want to use string instead of tape for this activity.

● **What was it like to act out an entire day while restricted by tape bands?**

● **How was acting out a day while bound by tape like living through a day bound by fear?**

● **Have you ever chosen not to do something because of fear? When? Why?**

When trios have finished, invite kids to share times they've felt paralyzed by fear. Then say: **If you let them, your fears can bind you like the tape bound you in this experience. But you don't have to let your fears paralyze you. <u>Prayer can free you from your fears.</u> Let's find out how.**

DIGGING IN ▼

LEADER TIP
for When I'm Afraid

If you don't have enough green markers for everyone, let kids use any bright-colored markers or crayons. They could write with red, orange, blue, purple, or any colors that will sharply contrast with the black they used earlier.

When I'm Afraid (10 to 12 minutes)

Say: **Many people in the Bible prayed to help them overcome their fears. The book of Psalms is a collection of prayers, and it includes prayers about many of the fears we've discussed today.**

Distribute copies of the "Psalms" Depthfinder (p. 43). Have each trio read the Depthfinder and select a psalm that addresses a fear all three members can relate to. Have trios read the psalms they've chosen and discuss the following questions:

● **How is this psalm like the prayers you pray when you're afraid? How is it different?**

● **How can you trust God with your fear?**

● **What's one thing you can learn from this psalm about praying when you're afraid?**

When trios have finished, say: **Stand next to one of the fears you wrote on the newsprint earlier.**

As kids find places to stand, give each student a green marker. Say: **Based on the psalm you've just read, free-write one way God can help you with your fear.**

Allow two minutes for kids to write their responses and then call the group together. Say: **<u>Prayer can free you from your fears.</u> People in biblical times used the psalms we just read as prayers to help them overcome their fears. We can use the psalms as prayers, too. For example, if you discover a psalm that addresses one of your fears, you could pray that psalm the next time you're afraid.**

Pray It! (10 to 12 minutes)

Say: **Based on the psalms we've read, let's create our own prayerful psalms to help us overcome our fears.**

Form four groups, and assign each group a separate wall. If you have more than sixteen students, assign several groups of four or fewer students to each wall.

Say: **In your group, write a prayer psalm about the fears listed on your wall. Write your psalm on the newsprint. Use the psalms listed on the handout as models. Start your psalm by expressing the fears on your wall as questions. For example, if "parents divorcing" is listed on your wall, you might write, "Why don't families stay together?" Then write expressions of trust in God, using the psalms as your example.**

As you write your psalms, use the black marker when referring to anything about fear and the green marker when referring to anything about trusting God.

Distribute green and black markers. As groups work, help them find psalms to use as models for their prayer psalms. Refer to the "Psalms" Depthfinder below for ideas.

When groups have finished, have them prepare unique ways to share their psalms with each other. For example, they might sing their psalms to a familiar tune or read their psalms from under a table as they "hide" from their fears. After each group presents its psalm, invite other kids to tell what they liked about it. Then ask the whole group:

● **How are the psalms you just wrote like the prayers you usually pray when you're afraid? How are they different?**

● **Will praying psalms like these help free you from your fears? Why or why not?**

Say: **Prayer can free you from your fears.** Let's pray about our fears now.

LEADER TIP
for Pray It!

Plan a time when your students can share their psalms in a worship service at your church. Encourage everyone to participate, but don't force anyone into doing it.

DEPTH FINDER   PSALMS

The book of Psalms is a book of prayers, and many of them were written when people felt afraid. When you feel afraid, pray a psalm! Here are psalms that correspond to some fears we feel today:

Fears	Psalms That Help Us Conquer Our Fears
Being betrayed by a friend	Psalm 55—God can keep us safe from people who betray us.
Being hurt or killed	Psalm 3—God can keep us safe from our enemies.
Being ridiculed for being a Christian	Psalm 43—God can defend us against those who don't believe in him.
Dying from diseases such as AIDS	Psalm 91—God can protect us from cancer and deadly diseases.
Dying in an earthquake, flood, fire, or any other natural disaster	Psalm 46—God can help us in the midst of earthquakes, flood, fires, and other disasters.
Failing in life	Psalm 37:1-19—God can look after those who trust him with their lives.
Losing someone to death or divorce	Psalm 27:7-10—God can take us in, even if we lose those we love.

Cut Loose (5 to 10 minutes) Have kids stand close together in a circle. Tie the end of a ball of string to the ankle of one student. Say: **We're going to take turns reading aloud all the fears written on the walls so we can pray about them. After you read a fear, wrap the string around your waist and toss the ball of string to someone across the circle. We'll keep reading and wrapping until we've read all the fears.**

When kids have read all the fears, everyone should be wrapped in the string. If not, allow kids to wrap and toss the string a few more times until everyone is wrapped in it. Say: **Today you talked about ways your fears surround and bind you. But prayer can free you from your fears. Let's pray about your fears right now.**

Invite volunteers to pray that everyone in the group would be freed from fear. Or allow kids to pray silently about their own fears. Then read one verse aloud from the following list: Deuteronomy 31:6, 8; Psalm 3:3, 6; Psalm 27:1-3; Psalm 118:5-6; Isaiah 41:13; and John 14:27. After you read one verse, cut one student free from the web of string. Then have that student read another verse from the list and cut free one or two more people. Continue until everyone has been cut free. If kids have read all the verses on the list and some students are still tied in string, have kids reread verses from the list until everyone is free.

Say: **God wants to free you from your fears. The Bible says that perfect love casts out fear. If you pray and trust God, God will take your fears away.**

DEPTH FINDER — UNDERSTANDING THESE KIDS

"I'm afraid of being a bum when I grow up. I want to at least have a good job—the real world scares me."

"I'm scared that death will take someone in my close family or one of my best friends."

"I'm afraid of having a hospital death, hooked up on machines."

Those are real-life fears of real-life teenagers. We interviewed over fifty teenagers about their three biggest fears. Their responses ranged from that of sharks to public speaking to losing control of themselves. The three fears mentioned most were

1. fear of not making it in life,
2. fear of family members or friends dying, and
3. fear of dying themselves, especially in an unnatural way.

Other common fears included those of failure, spiders, fire, losing hope, violence, falling, and disappointing parents or other respected adults.

Tearing Down the Fears

(up to 5 minutes)

Say: **Earlier we discovered how fear can wrap us up and restrict us. Now that we've given our fears to God in prayer, let's tear down our fears and wrap them up to show that they no longer control us.**

Have kids tear the newsprint from the walls. Encourage them to tear out one or more of their fears and wad them into a ball. Then have kids return to their original trios. Distribute masking tape, and say: **Earlier we wrapped each other up with this tape to represent our fears. To help us remember that prayer can free us from our fears, let's wrap each other's fears with God's love and protection. Wrap each person's fear with tape and then read 2 Timothy 1:7 to each other. Say the name of the person whose fear you've wrapped and then read the verse as if it were written directly to that person. For example, you might say, "Anthony, God did not give you a spirit that makes you afraid but a spirit of power and love and self-control."**

When kids have finished, say: **Prayer can free you from your fears. When you give your fears to God, he'll give you a spirit of power to help you overcome them. Take a moment now and tell the other people in your trio about times they've shown a spirit of power. For example, maybe someone in your group defended a friend who was picked on. Or maybe someone said no to pressure to drink or take drugs.** If the kids in your group don't know each other well, have each person come up with his or her own example. Then invite trio members to congratulate each other for being strong in the face of fear.

As kids encourage each other, set a basket near the door. The basket should be large enough to hold everyone's fear balls. As kids leave, say: **Remember that prayer can free you from your fears. You may wish to make a commitment today to pray every time you feel fear. As you leave, you may toss your fear into the basket as a symbol of releasing your fear to God and of your commitment to pray whenever you feel afraid.**

LEADER TIP

for Tearing Down the Fears

If you have a large class, you can save time by having kids wrap up their own "fear balls" and read the verse to each other. Or you can skip the tape and just have kids wad up their fears.

HeLP IS ON THE WAY

Equipping Kids
to Become
Answers to
Prayer

BY BOB BULLER

■ If you were to ask the teenagers in your group how many of them believe that God answers prayer, chances are that most, if not all, of them would raise their hands. Like most Christians, the kids in your group pray because they believe (at least, most of the time) that God hears and answers them. Granted, the answer God gives them may not be the one they had hoped for, but they still believe that God answers each and every prayer in his own wise and loving way. ■ What would happen, however, if you asked the kids in your group *how* God answers prayer? What sort of answer would you get to that question? In all probability, some kids would explain that God simply decides what he wants to do and then does it. The fact is, many Christians seem to assume that God is the only one involved in answering prayer. ■ According to the Bible, that assumption is false. Ultimately, God is the one who answers prayers, but God has also given Christians an important part to play in the process. For example, although God can miraculously feed the hungry and clothe those who need it, he usually relies on his people to meet those basic human needs for others (see Matthew 25:34-45). God expects *us* to become answers to prayer by serving and meeting the needs of others. ■ This study will help your kids discover their opportunity and responsibility to become answers to prayer. In so doing, it will motivate your kids to accomplish God's will on earth by serving and meeting the needs of others.

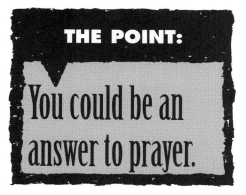

THE POINT:

You could be an answer to prayer.

The Study
AT A GLANCE

SECTION	MINUTES	WHAT STUDENTS WILL DO	SUPPLIES
Opening Experience	10 to 15	NO ANSWER—Discuss a true story about starvation.	
Bible Discovery	20 to 25	VARIOUS NEEDS, VARIOUS ANSWERS—Rewrite Bible passages to show what might have happened if certain people had refused to serve others.	Bibles, paper, pens
Life Application	10 to 15	WE ARE HIS HANDS—List and choose needs they could meet.	Latex gloves, newsprint, tape, markers
Closing Commitment	up to 5	THE RIGHT ANSWER—Commit to meeting a need.	

notes:

You could be an answer to prayer.

THE BIBLE CONNECTION

1 KINGS 17:7-16	God provided food for the widow at Zarephath.
JOB 1:13-19 and 2:11-13	Job's friends helped him deal with his grief by coming to be with him, sitting with him, and silently allowing him to mourn.
LUKE 10:30-37	The Good Samaritan showed love for his neighbor by taking care of his physical and financial needs.
ACTS 10:1-23	Peter answered Cornelius' prayers to God by going to him and telling him about God's gift of eternal life through Jesus Christ.
JAMES 2:14-17	James teaches that only genuine faith that is evidenced through action proves a person's claim to be a Christian.

In this study, kids will discuss a true story about a prayer need, examine how God met the needs of people in the Bible, and commit to meeting the specific needs of others.

Through this experience, kids can discover that they have an opportunity and a responsibility to become answers to prayer.

Explore the verses in The Bible Connection, then examine the information in the Depthfinder boxes throughout the study to gain a deeper understanding of how these Scriptures connect with your young people.

BEFORE THE STUDY

For the "We Are His Hands" activity, inflate and tie off latex gloves so that they look like hands. You'll need one "hand" for each student in your group.

LEADER TIP for The Study

Because this topic can be so powerful and relevant to kids' lives, your group members may be tempted to get caught up in issues and lose sight of the deeper biblical principle found in The Point. Help your kids grasp The Point by guiding them to focus on the biblical investigation and discussing how God's truth connects with reality in their lives.

THE STUDY

OPENING EXPERIENCE ▼

No Answer (10 to 15 minutes)
Have kids form groups of four or five. Ask kids to spend thirty seconds telling their group members about one answer to prayer they have experienced or know about. Encourage kids to tell specifically what they prayed for and how God answered the prayer.

After a few minutes, ask for volunteers to report some of their groups' stories. Then say: **These stories and thousands of others like them demonstrate that prayer is a powerful force in our world. God has given us the privilege of praying to him for whatever we need, no matter how large or how small. God hears the small and large requests—but does he always answer them? I'd like you to listen to a true story W. Stanley Mooneyham tells of one Christian whose prayers didn't seem to be getting answered.**

Read aloud the "A Matter of Life and Death" Depthfinder on page 51. Then ask:

- **What do you think the mother's prayers are like?**
- **Do you believe that God can answer the mother's prayers?**
- **How could God answer the mother's prayers?**

Say: **God has given us the privilege and responsibility of reaching out to people like the family in the story I read. With your group, I'd like you to talk about ways God could use people to answer the mother's prayer. Discuss how God could use each of the following people to help the family. In your discussion, explain**

DEPTHFINDER UNDERSTANDING THE BIBLE

Some people have suggested that the teaching of James 2:14-17 (and the larger context of James 2:18-26) contradicts Paul's teaching that we are justified by faith apart from works (Romans 3:28). However, the contradiction is more perceived than real.

In Romans 3, Paul explains how a person becomes a Christian. In James 2, James discusses how someone can validate a *claim* to have faith. James states his thesis several times (James 2:14, 20, 24, and 26), and, although he words it differently each time, the gist remains the same: *Claims* to have faith mean nothing. The only thing that matters is genuine faith that shows itself in good deeds.

The relevance of James' teaching for this study should be apparent. Kind words are nice, but they're useless when unaccompanied by kind actions. Praying for the needs of others is nice, but doing so doesn't validate one's claim to be a Christian. True Christians pray for *and* meet the needs of others.

what it would take to get the person or people involved, what the person or people could do, and if you think the person or people will really take action.

Have groups discuss each of the following people:
- the narrator of the story,
- the other people in the village,
- a hunger-relief organization,
- our church,
- our youth group, and
- you.

Have kids come back together. Allow groups a minute or two to explain what they discussed. Ask:

- **What might prevent these people from taking action for this family?**

- **What will happen to the family if no one takes action?**

- **How could you be an answer to prayer for this family? for other people?**

- **What things prevent you from being an answer to prayer?**

- **Why does God use people to answer other people's prayers?**

Say: **Prayer is a powerful force in the world, but that doesn't mean that all our prayers will be answered as we want. Sometimes, for reasons known only to him, God says "no" to our requests. Sometimes God makes us wait before he answers our prayers. And sometimes God wants us to be answers to prayer. So today we're going to learn how <u>you could be an answer to prayer</u>.**

LEADER TIP for The Study

Whenever groups discuss a list of questions, write the questions on newsprint and tape the newsprint to the wall so groups can discuss the questions at their own pace.

DEPTH FINDER
A MATTER OF LIFE AND DEATH

It is a very bad year for Singhali, and the prospects for many families range from bleak to hopeless. I talked to one family for which hope has almost run out. The father's name is Gokal Whalji Christie. (The "Christie" part, I am told, was added to indicate their new faith when the family became Christian.) He is forty. His wife's name is Daruben. She is thirty. There are four children; the oldest son is twelve and has been dumb since birth.

Gokal is a laborer, but he has had no work for more than six months. In normal times his family would have two meals a day. Now they are thankful when they have one. Meal? Well, hardly. In the morning it's a cup of plain tea, no milk or sugar. In the afternoon—if there is an afternoon meal—it's a small millet cake *(bajari)* with tea and maybe a raw onion or other vegetable. This is not enough calories—less than a hundred—for bare survival, much less for work.

Tears fill the eyes of the mother as she says: "The children cry much of the time because they are hungry. It is hard for us not to weep with them. For the next crop we will have to wait one more year. If God keeps us alive, we will remain alive. Otherwise we will go back to God, and that is what I expect."

For the first time in my life I am face-to-face with a fellow Christian who fully expects to die—soon—from starvation.

Excerpted from W. Stanley Mooneyham, *What Do You Say to a Hungry World?*

Various Needs, Various Answers

(20 to 25 minutes)

Say: **Helping and serving others is vitally important. Let's look at the Bible to learn what God has to say about our responsibility to answer others' prayers by serving them.**

Have kids return to their groups from the opening. Instruct each group to read James 2:14-17 together and then discuss the following questions:

● **What does this passage say about how we should respond to the needs we see?**

● **What responsibility do we have to serve others? to help meet needs we know about?**

● **What does this passage say about Christians who don't meet the needs they see?**

Ask for volunteers to report their groups' answers. Then say: **According to the Bible, not only _could_ you be an answer to prayer but you _should_ be an answer to prayer. God expects you and me to help answer the prayers of needy people by serving them. But how can we do this? There are so many people with so many needs that we can't possibly serve them all...or can we? Let's see what God's Word says about the different ways we can be an answer to prayer by serving others.**

Assign one of the following passages to each group: 1 Kings 17:7-16; Job 1:13-19 and 2:11-13; Luke 10:30-37; and Acts 10:1-23. (If you have

"Suppose a brother or sister is without clothes and daily food. If one of you says to him, '**Go, I wish you well; keep warm and well fed,**' but does nothing about his physical needs, what good is it?"

—JAMES 2:15-16

more than four groups, assign two groups the same passage.) Instruct each group to read its passage and then discuss the following questions:

● **What need or prayer request is described in this passage?**

● **Who met this person's need or answered the request?**

● **How were God's people involved in meeting the need?**

Allow several minutes for reading and discussion and then give each group a sheet of paper and a pen. Inform groups that they have five minutes to rewrite the endings of their Bible stories to describe what could have happened if God's "helpers" had chosen not to act. Encourage group members to be sure everyone will be involved either as a story-creator, a recorder, or a reader.

After five minutes, have groups first read their passages and then read their alternate endings. When all the groups have presented their stories, ask:

● **What are the different types of needs described in these stories?**

● **What are the different ways God used someone to meet those needs?**

● **How do you think these acts of service were actually answers to prayer?**

● **What does this teach us about ways God can use us to answer prayers?**

● **What does this teach about the importance of meeting the needs of others?**

● **What might happen if we don't answer others' prayers by serving them?**

Say: **These stories teach that <u>you could be an answer to prayer</u> in various ways—by feeding the hungry, by comforting the lonely, by caring for the hurting, by taking the gospel to those who need it, and by praying for those whom only God can help.**

DEPTH FINDER — UNDERSTANDING OUR RESPONSIBILITY

Sometimes Christians become so focused on their own needs that they ignore the serious needs of others. But those with needs can share God's love by serving others, as evidenced in this story told by Mother Teresa as found in the September 14, 1997 issue of The Denver Post.

"One night a man came to our house and told me, 'There is a family with eight children. They have not eaten for days.' I took some food with me and went. When I came to that family, I saw the faces of those little children disfigured by hunger. I gave the rice to the mother. She divided the rice in two and went out, carrying half the rice. When she came back, I asked her, 'Where did you go?' She gave me this simple answer, 'To my neighbors; they are hungry also!'

"If our poor die of hunger, it is not because God does not care for them. Rather, it is because neither you nor I are generous enough. It is because we are not instruments of love in the hands of God. We do not recognize Christ when once again he appears to us in the hungry man, in the lonely woman, or in the child who is looking for a place to get warm."

LEADER TIP for We Are His Hands

Consider using hypoallergenic latex gloves for this activity. Some people are dangerously allergic to the powder on latex gloves.

LEADER TIP for We Are His Hands

If you don't want to use latex gloves, you can use cotton gloves stuffed with newspaper.

LIFE APPLICATION ▼

We Are His Hands

(10 to 15 minutes) Give everyone one of the inflated latex gloves you prepared before the study. Give each group a marker.

Hang a sheet of newsprint where everyone can see it. Then ask kids to call out specific needs that they know other people have. Encourage kids to call out needs of people in other nations, your community, their schools, and even your group—but without infringing upon anyone's privacy. Record kids' ideas on the sheet of newsprint.

After you've listed ten to fifteen needs, challenge kids each to choose one need they would like to meet in some way. After a minute of think time, have kids write the needs on the backs of their gloves and then share with their group members which needs they chose. Then have group members help each other think of two or three ways each person could serve the needy person he or she chose. Have kids write the ideas on the palms of their gloves.

Allow at least five minutes for discussion. Then say: **Mark Gersmehl, a Christian songwriter, once said that we are God's hands on this earth. We are God's hands to feed the hungry, to reach out to the lonely, to bandage and soothe the hurting, to carry the gospel to those who need to hear it, and to pray for** 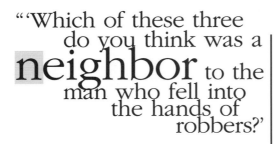 **those who need God's special help. You are God's hands, and** <u>**you could be an answer to prayer**</u> **by stretching out your hands to serve those around you.**

" 'Which of these three do you think was a **neighbor** to the man who fell into the hands of robbers?'

The expert in the law replied, 'The one who had **mercy** on him.' "

—Luke 10:36-37a

DEPTH FINDER

UNDERSTANDING PRAYER

At times, Christians seem to do less than they should because they believe that God will accomplish his will regardless of what they do. This belief contains a nugget of truth, but it is not the whole truth. The Bible does teach that God is powerful enough to overcome any obstacle in the working out of his sovereign will.

But God's Word also teaches that Christians play an integral role in accomplishing God's specific will on earth. God expects *us* to feed the hungry, give water to the thirsty, open our homes to strangers, clothe those who need it, look after the sick, and visit those in prison. God will accomplish his ultimate purpose, which is to establish his reign over all creation. But God has given Christians the responsibility to spread his love on earth every day and in every possible way.

So can our disobedience thwart or block God's will on earth? Ultimately, no. God sovereignly rules over all creation. But at times, God seems to limit the working out of his specific will to our efforts. When we obey God and meet the needs of others, we accomplish God's will on earth. But if we disobey God and ignore the needs around us, God may permit those needs to go unmet.

CLOSING COMMITMENT ▼

The Right Answer (up to 5 minutes)

Ask kids to form a standing circle and then each place their left hands on the shoulders of the people to their left while holding their glove-hands up to God with their right hands.

Challenge kids to each silently commit to God one thing they will do to serve the people represented on their glove-hands. Allow one minute for kids to make their commitments. Then close with a prayer asking God to use your kids to be answers to prayer by serving those they meet.

Let's Start With the Big Picture

Think back to a major life lesson you've learned.
Got it? Now answer these questions:
● Did you learn your lesson from something you read?
● Did you learn it from something you heard?
● Did you learn it from something you experienced?

If you're like 99 percent of your peers, you answered "yes" only to the third question—you learned your life lesson from something you experienced.

This simple test illustrates the most convincing reason for using active and interactive learning with young people: People learn best through experience. Or to put it even more simply, people learn by doing.

Learning by doing is what active learning is all about. No more sitting quietly in chairs and listening to a speaker expound theories about God—that's passive learning. Active learning gets kids out of their chairs and into the experience of life. With active learning, kids get to *do* what they're studying. They *feel* the effects of the principles you teach. They *learn* by experiencing truth firsthand.

Active learning works because it recognizes three basic learning needs and uses them in concert to enable young people to make discoveries on their own and to find practical life applications for the truths they believe.

So what are these three basic learning needs?
1. Teenagers need action.
2. Teenagers need to think.
3. Teenagers need to talk.

Read on to find out exactly how these needs will be met by using the active and interactive learning techniques in Group's Core Belief Bible Study Series in your youth group.

1. Teenagers Need Action

Aircraft pilots know well the difference between passive and active learning. Their passive learning comes through listening to flight instructors and reading flight-instruction books. Their active learning comes through actually flying an airplane or flight simulator. Books and lectures may be helpful, but pilots really learn to fly by manipulating a plane's controls themselves.

We can help young people learn in a similar way. Though we may engage students passively in some reading and listening to teachers, their understanding and application of God's Word will really take off through simulated and real-life experiences.

Forms of active learning include simulation games; role-plays; service projects; experiments; research projects; group pantomimes; mock trials; construction projects; purposeful games; field trips; and, of course, the most powerful form of active learning—real-life experiences.

We can more fully explain active learning by exploring four of its characteristics:

● **Active learning is an adventure.** Passive learning is almost always predictable. Students sit passively while the teacher or speaker follows a planned outline or script.

In active learning, kids may learn lessons the teacher never envisioned. Because the leader trusts students to help create the learning experience, learners may venture into unforeseen discoveries. And often the teacher learns as much as the students.

● **Active learning is fun and captivating.** What are we communicating when we say, "OK, the fun's over—time to talk about God"? What's the hidden message? That joy is separate from God? And that learning is separate from joy?

What a shame.

Active learning is not joyless. One seventh-grader we interviewed clearly remembered her best Sunday school lesson: "Jesus was the light, and we went into a dark room and shut off the lights. We had a candle, and we learned that Jesus is the light and the dark can't shut off the light." That's active learning. Deena enjoyed the lesson. She had fun. And she learned.

Active learning intrigues people. Whether they find a foot-washing experience captivating or maybe a bit uncomfortable, they learn. And they learn on a level deeper than any work sheet or teacher's lecture could ever reach.

● **Active learning involves everyone.** Here the difference between passive and active learning becomes abundantly clear. It's like the difference between watching a football game on television and actually playing in the game.

The "trust walk" provides a good example of involving everyone in active learning. Half of the group members put on blindfolds; the other half serve as guides. The "blind" people trust the guides to lead them through the building or outdoors. The guides prevent the blind people from falling down stairs or tripping over rocks. Everyone needs to participate to learn the inherent lessons of trust, faith, doubt, fear, confidence, and servanthood. Passive spectators of this experience would learn little, but participants learn a great deal.

● **Active learning is focused through debriefing.** Activity simply for activity's sake doesn't usually result in good learning. Debriefing— evaluating an experience by discussing it in pairs or small groups— helps focus the experience and draw out its meaning. Debriefing helps sort and order the information students gather during the experience. It helps learners relate the recently experienced activity to their lives.

The process of debriefing is best started immediately after an experience. We use a three-step process in debriefing: reflection, interpretation, and application.

Reflection—This first step asks the students, "How did you feel?" Active-learning experiences typically evoke an emotional reaction, so it's appropriate to begin debriefing at that level.

Some people ask, "What do feelings have to do with education?" Feelings have everything to do with education. Think back again to that time in your life when you learned a big lesson. In all likelihood, strong feelings accompanied that lesson. Our emotions tend to cement things into our memories.

When you're debriefing, use open-ended questions to probe feelings. Avoid questions that can be answered with a "yes" or "no." Let your learners know that there are no wrong answers to these "feeling" questions. Everyone's feelings are valid.

Interpretation—The next step in the debriefing process asks, "What does this mean to you? How is this experience like or unlike some other aspect of your life?" Now you're asking people to identify a message or principle from the experience.

You want your learners to discover the message for themselves. So instead of telling students your answers, take the time to ask questions that encourage self-discovery. Use Scripture and discussion in pairs or small groups to explore how the actions and effects of the activity might translate to their lives.

Alert! Some of your people may interpret wonderful messages that you never intended. That's not failure! That's the Holy Spirit at work. God allows us to catch different glimpses of his kingdom even when we all look through the same glass.

Application—The final debriefing step asks, "What will you do about it?" This step moves learning into action. Your young people have shared a common experience. They've discovered a principle. Now they must create something new with what they've just experienced and interpreted. They must integrate the message into their lives.

The application stage of debriefing calls for a decision. Ask your students how they'll change, how they'll grow, what they'll do as a result of your time together.

2. Teenagers Need to Think

Today's students have been trained not to think. They aren't dumber than previous generations. We've simply conditioned them not to use their heads.

You see, we've trained our kids to respond with the simplistic answers they think the teacher wants to hear. Fill-in-the-blank student workbooks and teachers who ask dead-end questions such as "What's the capital of Delaware?" have produced kids and adults who have learned not to think.

And it doesn't just happen in junior high or high school. Our children are schooled very early not to think. Teachers attempt to help kids read with nonsensical fill-in-the-blank drills, word scrambles, and missing-letter puzzles.

Helping teenagers think requires a paradigm shift in how we teach. We need to plan for and set aside time for higher-order thinking and be willing to reduce our time spent on lower-order parroting. Group's Core Belief Bible Study Series is designed to help you do just that.

Thinking classrooms look quite different from traditional classrooms. In most church environments, the teacher does most of the talking and hopes that knowledge will transmit from his or her brain to the students'. In thinking settings, the teacher coaches students to ponder, wonder, imagine, and problem-solve.

3. Teenagers Need to Talk

Everyone knows that the person who learns the most in any class is the teacher. Explaining a concept to someone else is usually more helpful to the explainer than to the listener. So why not let the students do more teaching? That's one of the chief benefits of letting kids do the talking. This process is called interactive learning.

What is interactive learning? Interactive learning occurs when students discuss and work cooperatively in pairs or small groups.

Interactive learning encourages learners to work together. It honors the fact that students can learn from one another, not just from the teacher. Students work together in pairs or small groups to accomplish shared goals. They build together, discuss together, and present together. They teach each other and learn from one another. Success as a group is celebrated. Positive interdependence promotes individual and group learning.

Interactive learning not only helps people learn but also helps learners feel better about themselves and get along better with others. It accomplishes these things more effectively than the independent or competitive methods.

Here's a selection of interactive learning techniques that are used in Group's Core Belief Bible Study Series. With any of these models, leaders may assign students to specific partners or small groups. This will maximize cooperation and learning by preventing all the "rowdies" from linking up. And it will allow for new friendships to form outside of established cliques.

Following any period of partner or small-group work, the leader may reconvene the entire class for large-group processing. During this time the teacher may ask for reports or discoveries from individuals or teams. This technique builds in accountability for the teacherless pairs and small groups.

Pair-Share—With this technique each student turns to a partner and responds to a question or problem from the teacher or leader. Every learner responds. There are no passive observers. The teacher may then ask people to share their partners' responses.

Study Partners—Most curricula and most teachers call for Scripture passages to be read to the whole class by one person. One reads; the others doze.

Why not relinquish some teacher control and let partners read and react with each other? They'll all be involved—and will learn more.

Learning Groups—Students work together in small groups to create a model, design artwork, or study a passage or story; then they discuss what they learned through the experience. Each person in the learning group may be assigned a specific role. Here are some examples:

Reader

Recorder (makes notes of key thoughts expressed during the reading or discussion)

Checker (makes sure everyone understands and agrees with answers arrived at by the group)

Encourager (urges silent members to share their thoughts)

When everyone has a specific responsibility, knows what it is, and contributes to a small group, much is accomplished and much is learned.

Summary Partners—One student reads a paragraph, then the partner summarizes the paragraph or interprets its meaning. Partners alternate roles with each paragraph.

The paraphrasing technique also works well in discussions. Anyone who wishes to share a thought must first paraphrase what the previous person said. This sharpens listening skills and demonstrates the power of feedback communication.

Jigsaw—Each person in a small group examines a different concept, Scripture, or part of an issue. Then each teaches the others in the group. Thus, all members teach, and all must learn the others' discoveries. This technique is called a jigsaw because individuals are responsible to their group for different pieces of the puzzle.

JIGSAW EXAMPLE

Here's an example of a jigsaw.

Assign four-person teams. Have teammates each number off from one to four. Have all the Ones go to one corner of the room, all the Twos to another corner, and so on.

Tell team members they're responsible for learning information in their numbered corners and then for teaching their team members when they return to their original teams.

Give the following assignments to various groups:

Ones: Read Psalm 22. Discuss and list the prophecies made about Jesus.

Twos: Read Isaiah 52:13–53:12. Discuss and list the prophecies made about Jesus.

Threes: Read Matthew 27:1-32. Discuss and list the things that happened to Jesus.

Fours: Read Matthew 27:33-66. Discuss and list the things that happened to Jesus.

After the corner groups meet and discuss, instruct all learners to return to their original teams and report what they've learned. Then have each team determine which prophecies about Jesus were fulfilled in the passages from Matthew.

Call on various individuals in each team to report one or two prophecies that were fulfilled.

You Can Do It Too!

All this information may sound revolutionary to you, but it's really not. God has been using active and interactive learning to teach his people for generations. Just look at Abraham and Isaac, Jacob and Esau, Moses and the Israelites, Ruth and Boaz. And then there's Jesus, who used active learning all the time!

Group's Core Belief Bible Study Series makes it easy for you to use active and interactive learning with your group. The active and interactive elements are automatically built in! Just follow the outlines, and watch as your kids grow through experience and positive interaction with others.

FOR DEEPER STUDY

For more information on incorporating active and interactive learning into your work with teenagers, check out these resources:

● *Why Nobody Learns Much of Anything at Church: And How to Fix It,* by Thom and Joani Schultz (Group Publishing) and
● *Do It! Active Learning in Youth Ministry,* by Thom and Joani Schultz (Group Publishing).

your evaluation of

core belief

Bible Study Series
for junior high/middle school

the truth about
PRAYER

Group Publishing, Inc.
Attention: Core Belief Talk-Back
P.O. Box 481
Loveland, CO 80539
Fax: (970) 669-1994

Please help us continue to provide innovative and useful resources for ministry. After you've led the studies in this volume, take a moment to fill out this evaluation; then mail or fax it to us at the address above. Thanks!

• • • • • •

1. As a whole, this book has been (circle one)

not very helpful   very helpful
1   2   3   4   5   6   7   8   9   10

2. The best things about this book:

3. How this book could be improved:

4. What I will change because of this book:

5. Would you be interested in field-testing future Core Belief Bible Studies and giving us your feedback? If so, please complete the information below:

Name _____

Street address _____

City _____ State _____ Zip _____

Daytime telephone (____) _____ Date _____

THANKS!